CONIFEROUS FORESTS

ENDANGERED
BIOMES

DONNA LATHAM

Nomad Press
A division of Nomad Communications
10 9 8 7 6 5 4 3 2 1

Printed by Regal Printing Limited in China,
June 2011, Job Number 1105033
ISBN: 978-1-936313-55-6

Educational Consultant, Marla Conn

Questions regarding the ordering of this book should be addressed to
Independent Publishers Group
814 N. Franklin St.
Chicago, IL 60610
www.ipgbook.com

Nomad Press
2456 Christian St.
White River Junction, VT 05001
www.nomadpress.net

Image Credits

Corbisimages.com/ Scott Stulberg, cover; Michael T. Sedam, 26.

©iStockphoto.com/ Eric Isselée, Life on White, title page, 17, 28; Jay
Rysavy, 1; Jussi Santaniemi, 1; Valentin Casarsa, EyesOn, 3; AVTG, 5, 13,
15; Doug Cannell, Magnet Creative, 7; Katie Clarke, Opulent Images, 8; Phil
Augustavo, 9; Robert Blanchard, Catcher of Light Photography, 11; Dennis
Donohue, 11; Daniel Cardiff, 12; Anna Yu, AYImages, 12; Andy Gehrig, 12,
13, 20; StockstudioX, 12; Letty17, 13; Ziga Camernik, 14; Craftvision, 14;
David Mantel, 16; Boris Diakovsky, Boriail, 17; David Parsons, 18; Vassiliy
Vishnevskiy, 18; Don Wilkie, Wolverine Enterprises, 19, 26; Peter Zelei,
21; Nikolay Chsherbinin, 22; Patrick Robbins, Pivot, 22; Kyu Oh, 26.

CONTENTS

What Is a Biome?

Grab your backpack! You're about to embark on an exciting expedition to explore one of Earth's major **biomes**: the **coniferous forest**!

A biome is a large natural area with a distinctive **climate** and **geology**. The desert is a biome. The forest, ocean, and tundra are biomes. So is the coniferous forest. Biomes are the earth's communities.

Did You Know?

Scientists don't agree on how many biomes there are. Some divide the earth into five biomes. Others argue for 12.

biome: a large natural area with a distinctive climate, geology, and set of water resources. A biome's plants and animals are adapted for life there.

coniferous forest: a northern forest of trees.

climate: average weather patterns in an area over many years.

geology: the rocks, minerals, and physical structure of an area.

adapt: changes a plant or animal makes to survive in new or different conditions.

ecosystem: a community of living and nonliving things and their environment. Living things are plants, animals, and insects. Nonliving things are soil, rocks, and water.

environment: everything in nature, living and nonliving.

Each biome has its own biodiversity, which is the range of living things **adapted** for life there. It also contains many **ecosystems**. In an ecosystem, living and nonliving things interact with their **environment**.

Teamwork keeps the system balanced and working. Earth's biomes are connected together, creating a vast web of life.

2

Landscape and Climate

The coniferous forest is a vast band of trees that circles parts of Asia, Canada, Europe, Russia, and the United States. **Coniferous** trees, which don't shed their leaves each year, define the largest land biome on earth.

here: The coniferous forest climate has only two seasons. Long, dry winters are cold. Short, wet summers are cool.

there: The deciduous forest climate enjoys four distinct seasons. These are spring, summer, fall, and winter.

of the Coniferous Forest

It's like a gigantic green wreath around the **Northern Hemisphere**. At its southern edge, the coniferous forest mingles with **deciduous** forests. To the north, it merges with the treeless Arctic tundra.

Word Exploration

Conifer comes from the Latin word conus, which means "cone," and ferre, "to bear."

Words to Know

coniferous: describes trees and bushes that produce their seeds in cones. Many coniferous trees have needles for leaves.

Northern Hemisphere: the half of the earth north of the equator.

deciduous: describes trees and bushes that shed their leaves each year.

There are two types of coniferous forests. Trees in closed-canopy forests grow tightly together. They shade the mossy carpet of the forest floor. Trees in open-canopy forests are scattered and widely spaced. Instead of velvety mosses, gray-green **lichen** sprawl over the ground.

Winters are long and bitterly cold. Temperatures plunge to −40 degrees Fahrenheit or colder (−40 degrees Celsius).

lichen: patchy plants that grow on rocks, trees, and other surfaces.

precipitation: any falling moisture, such as rain or snow.

decompose: to break down or rot.

humus: decaying matter made from dead plants and animals. Humus supplies soil with nutrients and helps soil retain water.

nutrients: substances that living things need to live and grow.

Summers only get as high as 70 degrees Fahrenheit (21 degrees Celsius). A brief growing season of three to four months sneaks in during the warmer, wetter months. Total **precipitation** in a year is 12 to 33 inches (30 to 85 centimeters).

Because of cool temperatures, dead plants and animals **decompose** slowly. This means that the soil has little **humus**, so it is low in **nutrients** for plants.

Lakes and swampy areas such as marshes and bogs cut through the coniferous forests. These wet places are perfect homes for millions and millions of insects.

6

Plants Growing in the

Conifers are cone-bearing trees. Cones hold seeds and scaly needles. Many conifers, also called **evergreens**, remain green all year round. Evergreens that thrive in the coniferous forest include cedar, cypress, fir, pine, and spruce. Hardy deciduous trees, such as aspen, poplar, and birch, squeeze in here and there.

How do conifers adapt to survive long, dry winters?

Deep, dark-green coloring helps evergreens capture lots of the sun's light for **photosynthesis**. A waxy coating on their needles protects them from drying out in winter winds.

Words to Know

evergreen: a tree that keeps its leaves or needles throughout the year.

photosynthesis: the process through which plants create food, using light as a source of energy.

Coniferous Forest Have Adapted

Did You Know?

You'll find some deciduous trees in the coniferous forest and some coniferous trees in the deciduous forest. But mostly conifers live in the coniferous forest. Mostly deciduous trees live in the deciduous forest.

Evergreens must use every minute of the brief growing season. So they cling to their needles all year. They don't have time to sprout new leaves and needles each year. When warmer weather and summer rains finally arrive, evergreens are all ready to start up photosynthesis.

These trees are pointed and narrow at the top and wide and full at the bottom. Thanks to this cone shape, snow swooshes off an evergreen's branches like a snowboard off a slope. This adaptation means snow doesn't pile up and crack branches under its heavy load.

Other plants, such as the sundew and pitcher plant have extreme adaptations for survival. These plants trap and gobble up insects to take in nutrients.

Did You Know?

The world's oldest living thing just happens to be a conifer, although it doesn't live in the coniferous forest. Ancient Methuselah is a bristlecone pine that grows in California's White Mountains. It is as old as the pyramids of Egypt. Scientists keep the exact location a secret because they are afraid someone might try to snip a souvenir from the tree.

Animals Living in the

During the short summer months, there is plenty of food in the coniferous forest. Many birds nest there, spending their time feeding on the vast insect population.

Woodpeck

Plants provide plenty to munch on too, for elk and moose, woodpeckers and ravens. Peregrine falcons swoop from rocky ledges to snatch their dinner in mid-air.

Siberian tiger

What Eats What?

Hungry **herbivores,** including elk, muskrats, and snowshoe hares, pluck juicy treats from blackberry bushes. Many animals of the coniferous forest are **carnivores**. These **predators**, such as Siberian tigers, grizzly bears, lynx, wolverines, and wolves, feast on plentiful **prey**.

Coniferous Forest
Have Adapted

Raven

Peregrine falcon

Elk

Wolverine

Words to Know

herbivore: an animal that eats only plants.

carnivore: an animal that eats only other animals.

predator: an animal that hunts another animal for food.

prey: an animal hunted by a predator for food.

12

When winter blasts in, animals have to adapt.

Bears **hibernate**, taking a long winter nap. Many birds **migrate**, including the grosbeak, a finch with an extra-large, seed-snapping beak. They spend the winter in warmer climates to the south.

Grizzly bear

Grosbeak finch

The snowshoe hare trades its brown summer coat for a white one that blends in with snow. With this **camouflage**, it remains one hop ahead of the hungry lynx.

To maneuver in *deep* snow, both animals scramble on long legs. Their webbed paws are built-in snowshoes.

Lynx

Words to Know

hibernate: to sleep through the winter in a cave or underground.

migrate: to move from one environment to another when seasons change.

camouflage: the colors or patterns that allow a plant or animal to blend in with its environment.

Hare

14

Environmental Threats

Clearcut logging threatens the coniferous forest. To clear land for homes, farms, or business, people sometimes chop down nearly every tree in an area. Clearcut logging wipes out **habitats** and leads to soil **erosion**. The soil's top layers have all the nutrients. When the soil loses those layers, it loses its ability to grow plants.

Words to Know

habitat: a plant or animal's home.

erosion: when land is worn away by wind or water.

Clearcut logging

Fires, accidentally started by people or caused by nature, endanger coniferous forests. Drawn by the spectacular beauty of the forests, many writers, photographers, artists, hikers, and campers frequently visit this biome. Unfortunately, visitors are sometimes careless with campfires, which can lead to raging forest fires.

Red squirrel

In summer, lightning ignites wildfires, which are fueled by dry needles. Thick bark helps protect trees against scorching flames, but destruction can be widespread.

Word Exploration

The coniferous forest is also called the boreal forest or taiga. Boreal is a Greek word that means "north." Taiga is a Russian word meaning "swampy pine forest."

Sparrow

Biodiversity at Risk

There is limited biodiversity in the coniferous forest. Fewer **species** exist here than in other environments, including the rainforest and deciduous forest. Many of the species that live in this biome are furry animals. For centuries, people have hunted them for their striking **pelts** and tasty meat. **Overhunting** has placed many animals at risk of **extinction**.

The Siberian tiger is a rare species because trophy-hunters have killed so many of the big cats for their pelts. Others poached the powerful predators to use their bones and body parts in traditional Chinese medicine.

Red-tailed hawk

Words to Know

species: a type of animal or plant.

pelts: animal skins.

overhunting: hunting an animal in such great numbers that its population falls to low levels. It can cause extinction.

extinction: the death of an entire species so that it no longer exists.

Today, scientists believe fewer than 400 Siberian tigers remain in the wild. Musk deer and caribou have also been overhunted for antlers, skins, and meat. They are at risk too.

Caribou

Path to Extinction

Rare: Only a small number of the species is alive. Scientists are concerned about the future of the species.

Threatened: The species lives, but its numbers will likely continue to decline. It will probably become endangered.

Endangered: The species is in danger of extinction in the very near future.

Extinct in the Wild: Some members of the species live, but only in protected captivity and not out in the wild.

Extinct: The species has completely died out. It has disappeared from the planet.

The Future of the

Forest fires, overhunting, clearcut logging, and habitat destruction will continue to threaten coniferous forests.

People are increasingly aware of the delicate balance of life on Earth. Many are devoted to conserving our natural resources and preserving our biomes. What's one way to preserve this important biome? We can plant a coniferous tree to replace every tree that is chopped down.

National parks protect the natural beauty of our forests. Olympic National Park in Washington and Jasper National Park in Alberta, Canada, are just two in North America.

Visit them to enjoy the wondrous coniferous forest.

Olympic National Park

Coniferous Forest

Conservation Challenge

Think about what You can do to benefit the environment. What actions can you take? How can you inspire others to do the same?

Make a poster to illustrate the best way to protect and preserve forests when you build campfires.

What's the safest way to build a fire? You already know to use extreme care and to work with an adult. Use the enclosed pits provided by forest preserves, or construct a circle of rocks around a pit area. Keep the fire small, so it's easier to contain.

When you're ready to leave your campsite or picnic area, thoroughly drown the flames with a bucket of water. Stir the fire with a shovel and douse all glowing embers. Drown the fire a second time.

Don't forget to leave your campsite cleaner than you found it!

Glossary

adapt: changes a plant or animal makes to survive in new or different conditions.

biodiversity: the range of living things in an ecosystem.

biome: a large natural area with a distinctive climate, geology, and set of water resources. A biome's plants and animals are adapted for life there.

camouflage: the colors or patterns that allow a plant or animal to blend in with its environment.

carnivore: an animal that eats only other animals.

climate: average weather patterns in an area over many years.

coniferous: describes trees and bushes that produce their seeds in cones and do not lose their leaves each year. Many coniferous trees have needles for leaves.

coniferous forest: a northern forest of trees.

deciduous: describes trees and bushes that shed their leaves each year.

decompose: to break down or rot.

ecosystem: a community of living and nonliving things and their environment. Living things are plants, animals, and insects. Nonliving things are soil, rocks, and water.

environment: everything in nature, living and nonliving.

erosion: when land is worn away by wind or water.

evergreen: a tree that keeps its leaves or needles throughout the year.

extinction: the death of an entire species so that it no longer exists.

geology: the rocks, minerals, and physical structure of an area.

Glossary

habitat: a plant or animal's home.

herbivore: an animal that eats only plants.

hibernate: to sleep through the winter in a cave or underground.

humus: decaying matter made from dead plants and animals. Humus supplies soil with nutrients and helps soil retain water.

lichen: patchy plants that grow on rocks, trees, and other surfaces.

migrate: to move from one environment to another when seasons change.

Northern Hemisphere: the half of the earth north of the equator.

nutrients: substances that living things need to live and grow.

overhunting: hunting an animal in such great numbers that its population falls to low levels. It can cause extinction.

pelts: animal skins.

photosynthesis: the process through which plants create food, using light as a source of energy.

precipitation: any falling moisture, such as rain or snow.

predator: an animal that hunts another animal for food.

prey: an animal hunted by a predator for food.

species: a type of animal or plant.

Further Investigations

Cherry, Lynn. *How We Know What We Know About Our Changing Climate: Scientists and Kids Explore Global Warming.* Dawn Publications, 2008.

Latham, Donna. *Amazing Biome Projects You Can Build Yourself.* Nomad Press, 2009.

Reilly, Kathleen M. *Planet Earth: 25 Environmental Projects You Can Build Yourself.* Nomad Press, 2008.

Rothschild, David. *Earth Matters: An Encyclopedia of Ecology.* DK Publishing, 2008.

Smithsonian Institution National Museum of Natural History
www.mnh.si.edu
Washington, D.C.

US National Parks www.us-parks.com

Enchanted Learning, Biomes
www.enchantedlearning.com/biomes

Energy Efficiency and Renewable Energy
www.eere.energy.gov/kids

Geography for Kids www.kidsgeo.com

Inch in a Pinch: Saving the Earth
www.inchinapinch.com

Kids Do Ecology
www.kids.nceas.ucsb.edu

Library ThinkQuest
www.thinkquest.org

National Geographic Kids
www.kids.nationalgeographic.com

NOAA for Kids
www.oceanservice.noaa.gov/kids

Oceans for Youth
www.oceansforyouth.org

The Nature Conservancy
www.nature.org

World Wildlife Federation
www.panda.org

Index